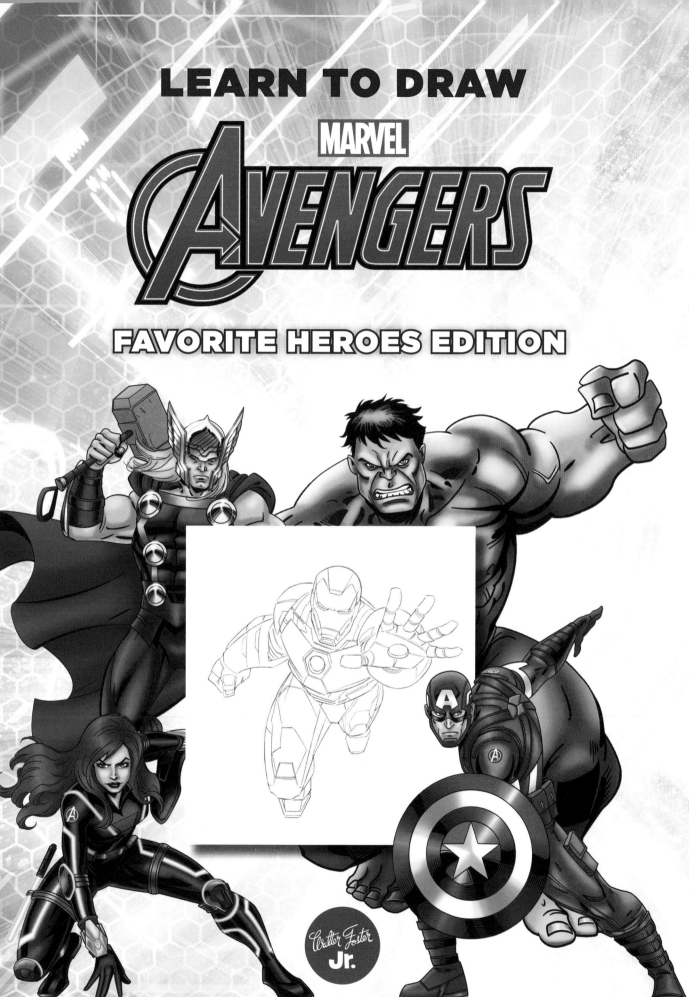

This library edition published in 2020 by Walter Foster Jr.,
an imprint of The Quarto Group
26391 Crown Valley Parkway, Suite 220
Mission Viejo, CA 92691, USA.

Character art by Cory Hamscher and Pablo Mendoza.
Photographs on pages 4-5 © 2007 Shutterstock.

Distributed in the United States and Canada by
Lerner Publisher Services
241 First Avenue North
Minneapolis, MN 55401 U.S.A.
www.lernerbooks.com

First Library Edition

Library of Congress Cataloging-in-Publication Data

Title: Learn to draw Marvel Avengers. Favorite heroes.
Description: First library edition. | Mission Viejo, CA : Walter Foster Jr.,
    an imprint of The Quarto Group, 2020. | Audience: Ages: 6+. | Audience:
    Grades: 4-6.
Identifiers: LCCN 2019017160 | ISBN 9781600588280 (hardcover)
Subjects: LCSH: Avengers (Fictitious characters)--Juvenile literature. |
    Superheroes in art--Juvenile literature. | Drawing--Technique--Juvenile
    literature.
Classification: LCC NC1764.8.H47 L4254 2020 | DDC 741.5/1--dc23 LC record available
at https://lccn.loc.gov/2019017160

Printed in USA
9 8 7 6 5 4 3 2 1

TABLE OF CONTENTS

TOOLS & MATERIALS

You need to gather only a few simple art supplies before you begin. Start with a drawing pencil and an eraser. Make sure you also have a pencil sharpener and a ruler. To add color to your drawings, use markers, colored pencils, crayons, watercolors, or acrylic paint. The choice is yours!

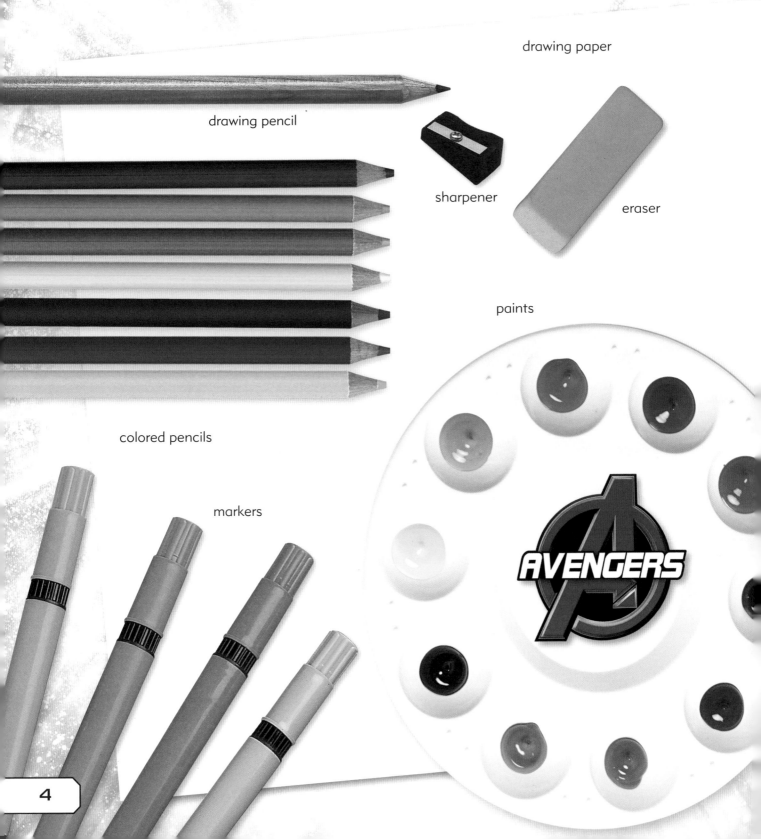

drawing paper

drawing pencil

sharpener

eraser

paints

colored pencils

markers

AVENGERS

paintbrushes

5

BASIC SHAPES DRAWING METHOD

When using the step-by-step drawing method, you will begin by drawing very basic shapes, such as lines and circles.

1

2

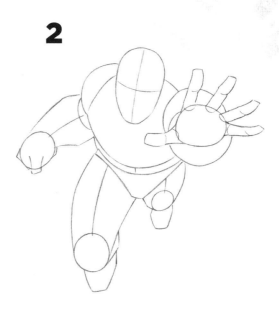

First draw the basic shapes, using light lines that will be easy to erase.

Pay attention to the new lines added in each step.

3

Erase guidelines and add more detail.

4

In each new step, add
more defining lines.

5

Take your time adding detail
and copying what you see.

6

Add color to your drawing
with colored pencils,
markers, paints, or crayons!

When inking, use different line weights and textures to define the shapes and the image as a whole. Fill in entire shapes in certain areas, such as the hair or legs, to emphasize the shadows. To show changes from solid black shadows to lighter areas, use hatching, crosshatching, or "feathered" brushstrokes or pen strokes.

Thin line weight

Thick line weight

Filled-in area

COLORING TECHNIQUES

You can color your drawings any way you'd like, using colored pencils, markers, or paints.

You can color the Hulk using one shade of green and one shade of purple, and he will definitely look like the Hulk. But if you want to take coloring to the next level, pay more attention to shadows and highlights.

See how in this second example, the Hulk looks more three-dimensional? This is because the lighter and darker areas bring out the Hulk's form. Pay attention to the final color steps in this book and try to copy the shadows and highlights in your coloring.

IRON MAN

Billionaire businessman Tony Stark was wounded, captured, and told to build a weapon by his enemies. But instead, Tony created an advanced suit of armor to heal his wounds and escape captivity. Now with a new outlook on life, Tony uses his money and intelligence to make the world a safer, better place as **Iron Man**.

REAL NAME:
Anthony "Tony" Stark

HEIGHT:
6'1" / 6'5" in armor

WEIGHT:
190 lbs. / 425 lbs. in armor

Powers & Abilities

- Invents advanced weapons, including new models of his Iron Man suit

- Flies using the suit

- Uses repulsor rays, pulse bolts, mini-missiles, magnetic field generators, and more while fighting his enemies

Follow along, first drawing basic shapes with light pencil lines. Copy the new lines shown in each step, eventually darkening the lines you want to keep and erasing the rest. Finally, add color to your drawing.

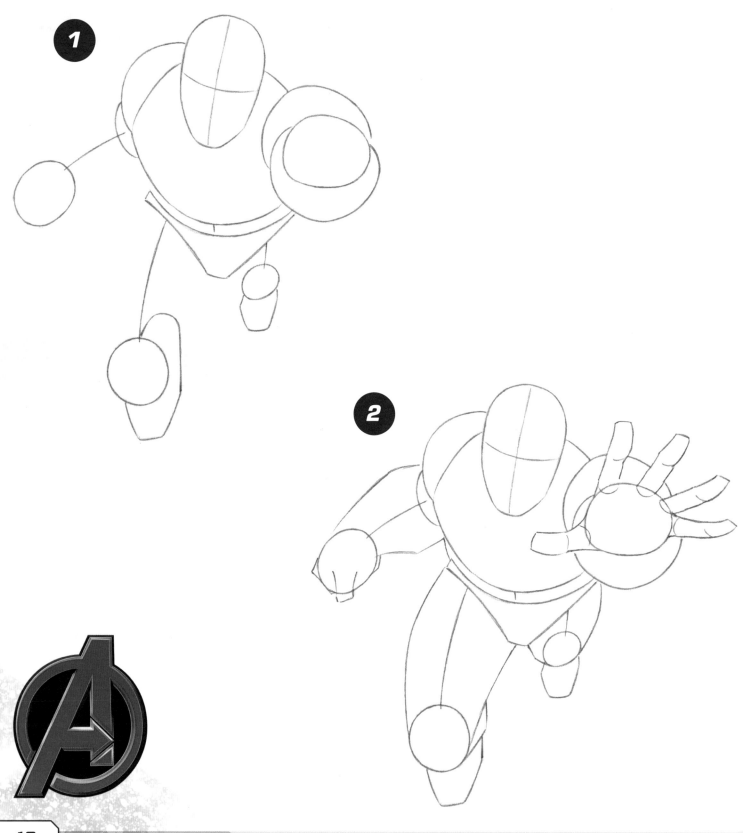

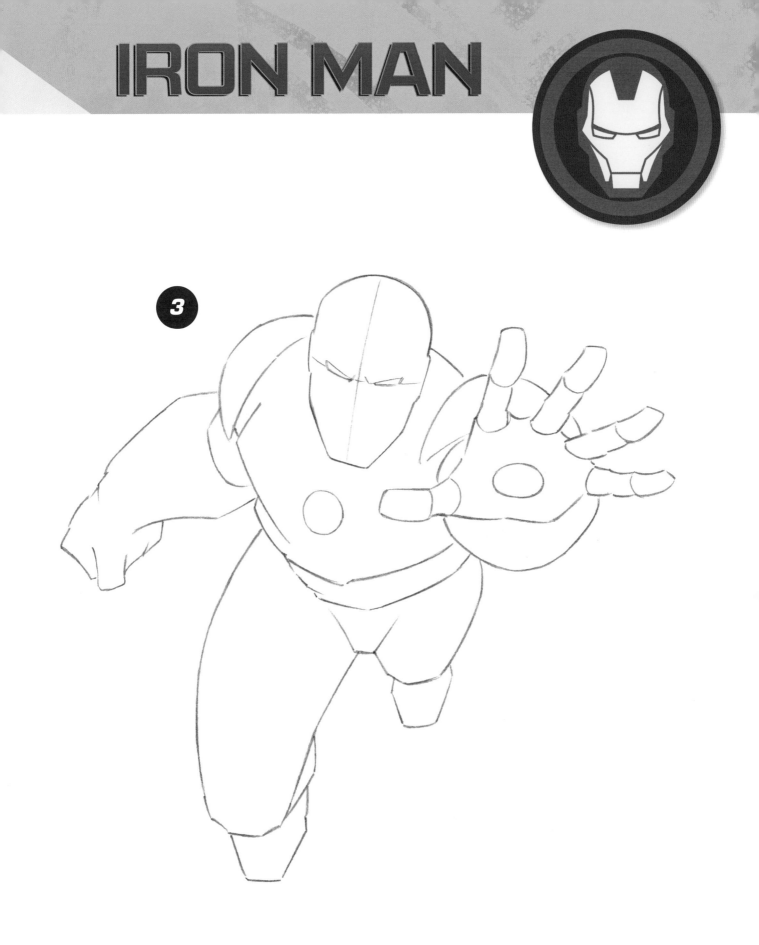

Tony entered MIT at 15 years old and graduated with two master's degrees by age 19. After graduation, Tony went to work for his father's company, Stark Industries.

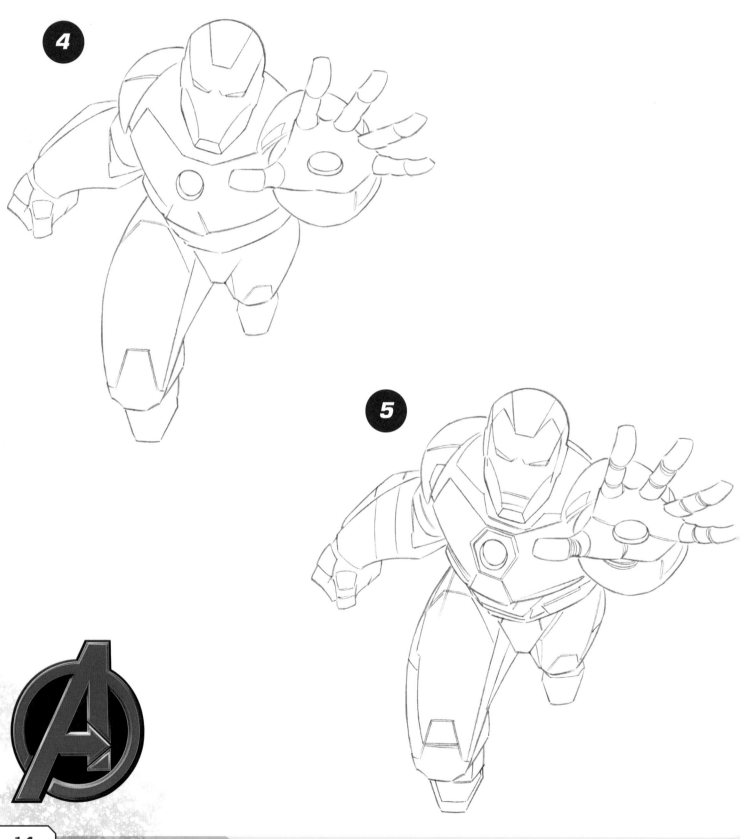

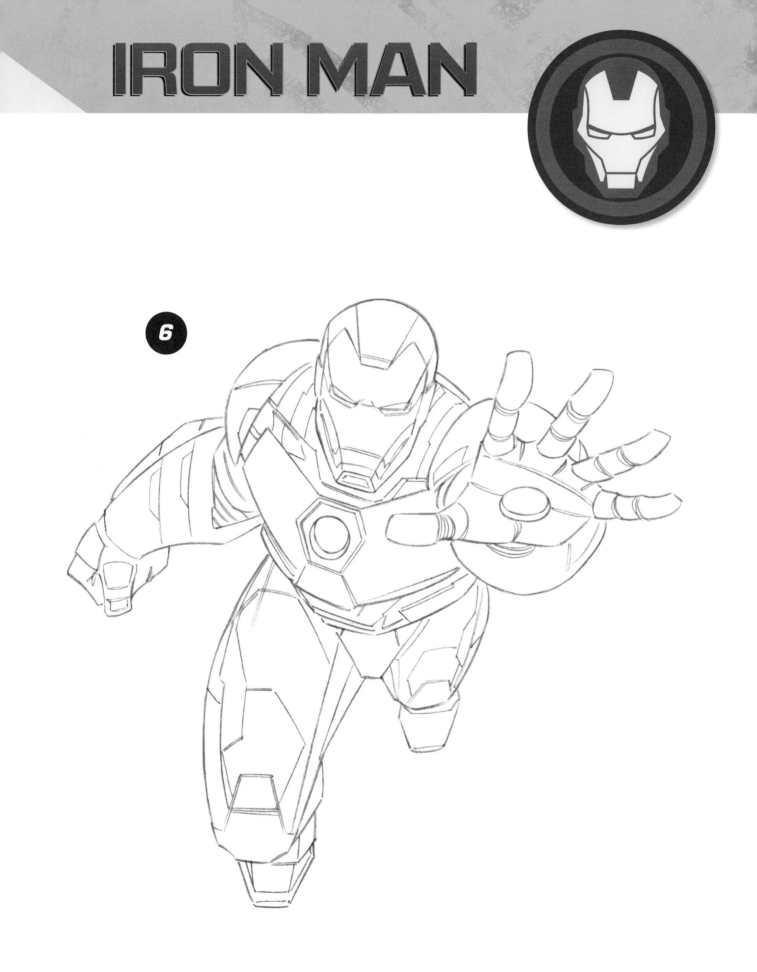

CAPTAIN AMERICA

Vowing to serve his country any way he could, young Steve Rogers took the Super-Soldier serum to become America's one-man army. Fighting for the red, white, and blue for more than 60 years, **Captain America** is the living, breathing symbol of freedom and liberty.

REAL NAME:
Steven "Steve" Rogers

HEIGHT:
6'2"

WEIGHT:
230 lbs.

Powers & Abilities

- Is more agile, stronger, and faster than regular soldiers

- Carries an indestructible shield that can also be used as a weapon

- Fights using his own style of hand-to-hand combat

Follow along, first drawing basic shapes with light pencil lines. Copy the new lines shown in each step, eventually darkening the lines you want to keep and erasing the rest. Finally, add color to your drawing.

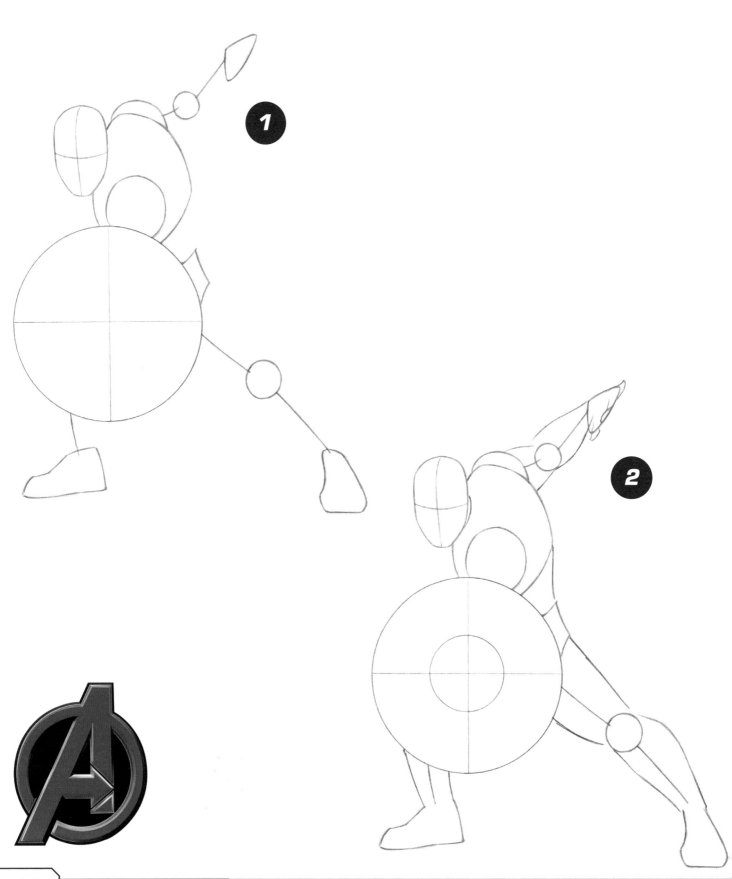

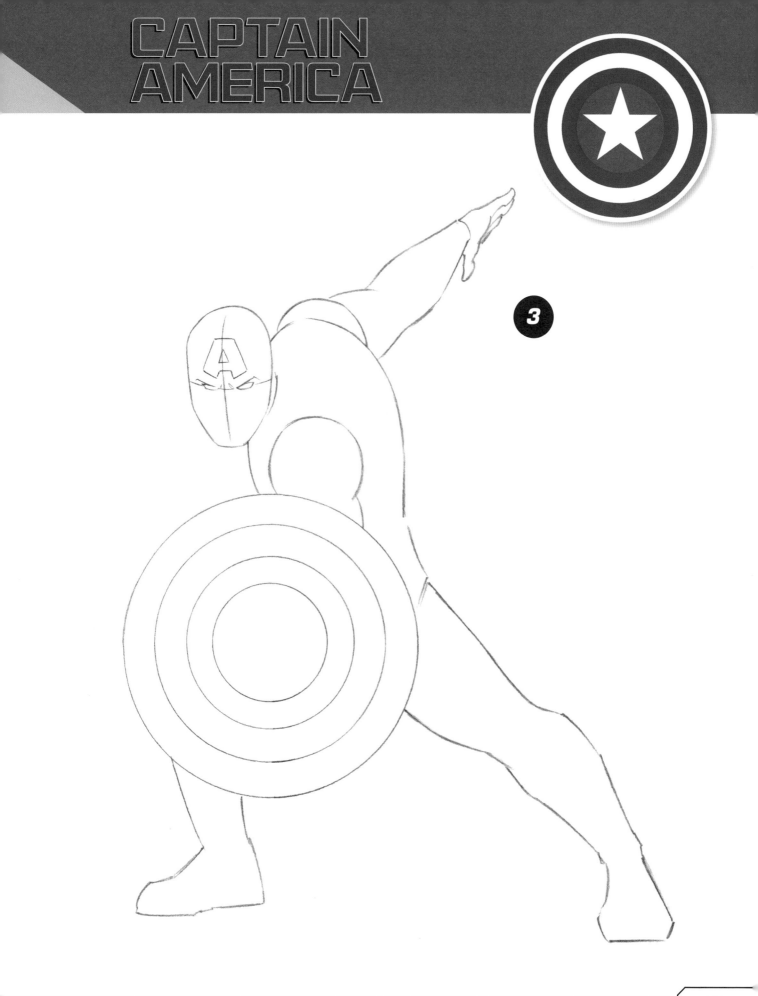

Captain America owes his powers and long life to Professor Abraham Erskine and Operation: Rebirth, a program that began during WWII to enhance U.S. soldiers.

6

8

FALCON

With a mental connection to all birds and a suit that gives him wings to fly, the **Falcon** has been both the partner to Captain America and an Avenger himself. Whether as a Super Hero or in his secret identity of social worker Sam Wilson, the Falcon dedicates his life to standing up for others.

REAL NAME:
Samuel Thomas "Sam" Wilson

HEIGHT:
6'0"

WEIGHT:
170 lbs.

Powers & Abilities

- Can telepathically communicate with birds and is able to receive mental images of what the birds see

  - Is highly trained in gymnastics and hand-to-hand combat

    - Wears a suit with glider wings that allow him to fly at speeds of more than 250 miles per hour

Follow along, first drawing basic shapes with light pencil lines. Copy the new lines
shown in each step, eventually darkening the lines you want to keep and erasing the rest.
Finally, add color to your drawing.

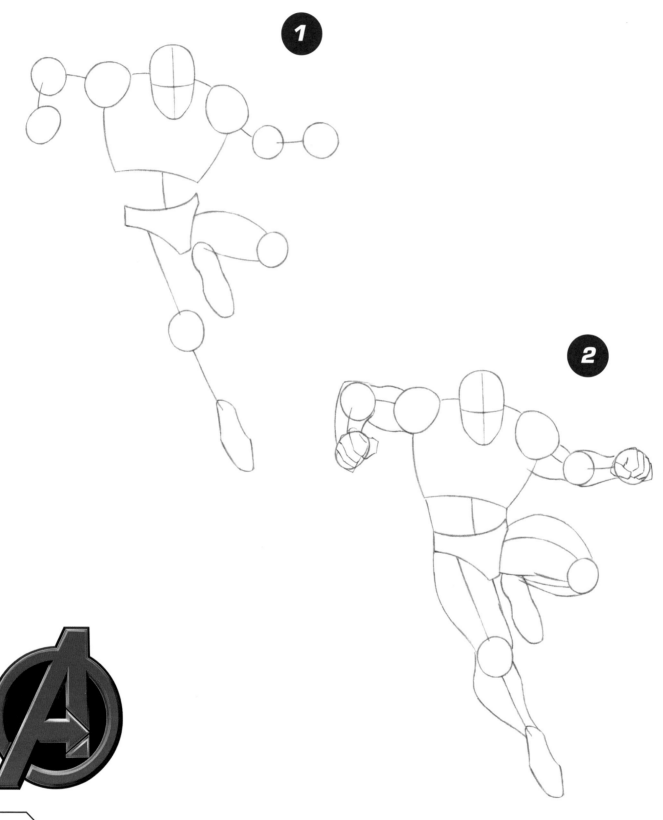

3

Sam, intelligent and adventurous, studied at S.H.I.E.L.D. and was at the top of his class.

FALCON

6

7

BLACK WIDOW

Natasha Romanoff is an expert spy, athlete, and assassin who goes by many aliases, including **Black Widow**. She started her training at an early age at the KGB's infamous Red Room Academy. Black Widow was formerly an enemy to the Avengers, but she later became their ally and a top S.H.I.E.L.D. agent.

REAL NAME:
Natalia "Natasha" Romanoff

HEIGHT:
5'7"

WEIGHT:
130 lbs.

Powers & Abilities

- Is an excellent fighter and spy due to her training

- Discharges the "widow's bite," high-frequency electrostatic bolts, from her bracelets

- Carries plastic explosive discs, knives, and other weapons in her protective suit

Follow along, first drawing basic shapes with light pencil lines. Copy the new lines shown in each step, eventually darkening the lines you want to keep and erasing the rest. Finally, add color to your drawing.

1

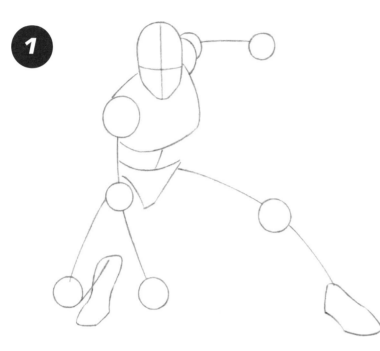

2

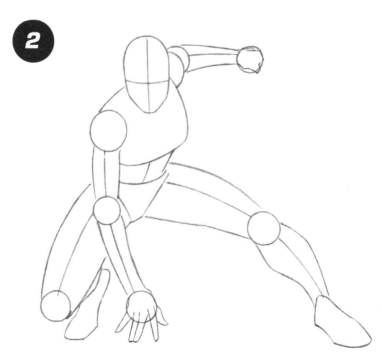

Natasha studied as a ballerina to cover for her true occupation,
a sleeper agent who spied on the United States.

4

5

6

Natasha's connection with Hawkeye led her to defect from her original keepers and right the wrongs of her past by joining S.H.I.E.L.D., which eventually led her to join the Avengers.

HAWKEYE

Clint Barton is the best archer ever known. After seeing Iron Man in action, he was inspired to become a costumed crime-fighter himself. He met his longtime friend Black Widow before joining the Avengers team as **Hawkeye**.

REAL NAME:
Clinton Francis "Clint" Barton

HEIGHT:
6'0"

WEIGHT:
185 lbs.

Powers & Abilities

- Is a world-class archer and marksman

- Throws knives, darts, boomerangs, and more

- Fights using hand-to-hand combat as well, thanks to his training with Captain America

- Pilots the Avengers' supersonic Quinjets and other aircraft

Follow along, first drawing basic shapes with light pencil lines. Copy the new lines shown in each step, eventually darkening the lines you want to keep and erasing the rest. Finally, add color to your drawing.

4

5

6

7

8

HULK

After being exposed to harmful gamma rays, Dr. Bruce Banner was transformed into the incredibly powerful creature called the **Hulk**. Dr. Bruce Banner is a genius in nuclear physics, but when he is the Hulk, Banner's consciousness is buried within the Hulk's.

REAL NAME:
Robert Bruce Banner

HEIGHT:
5'9" / 8'5" as Hulk

WEIGHT:
145 lbs. / 1,040 lbs. as Hulk

Powers & Abilities

• Becomes stronger and stronger as his stress level increases

• Leaps great distances

• Creates shock waves by slamming his hands together; this shock wave can deafen people, send objects flying, and extinguish fires

Follow along, first drawing basic shapes with light pencil lines. Copy the new lines shown in each step, eventually darkening the lines you want to keep and erasing the rest. Finally, add color to your drawing.

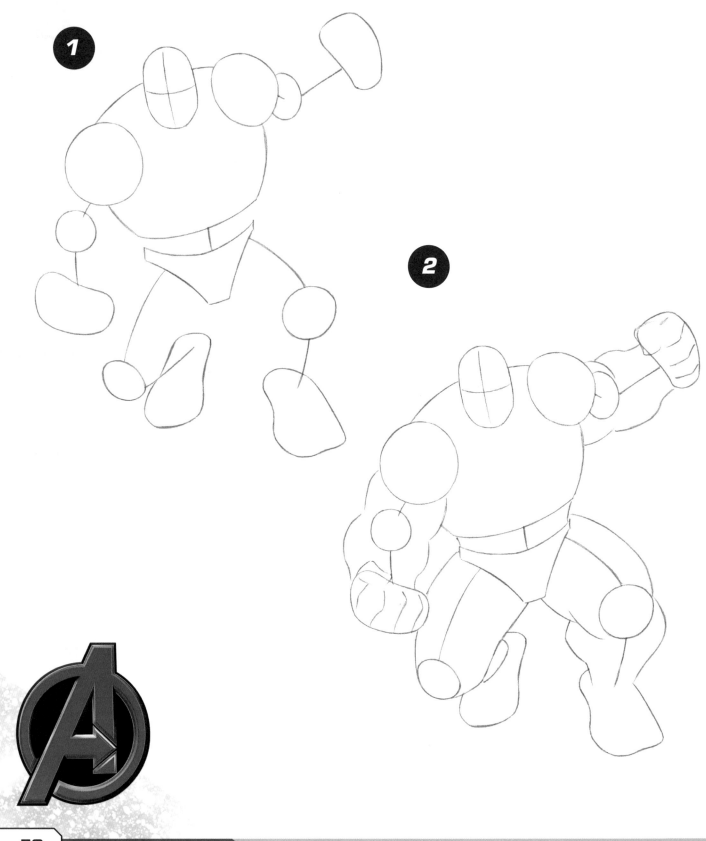

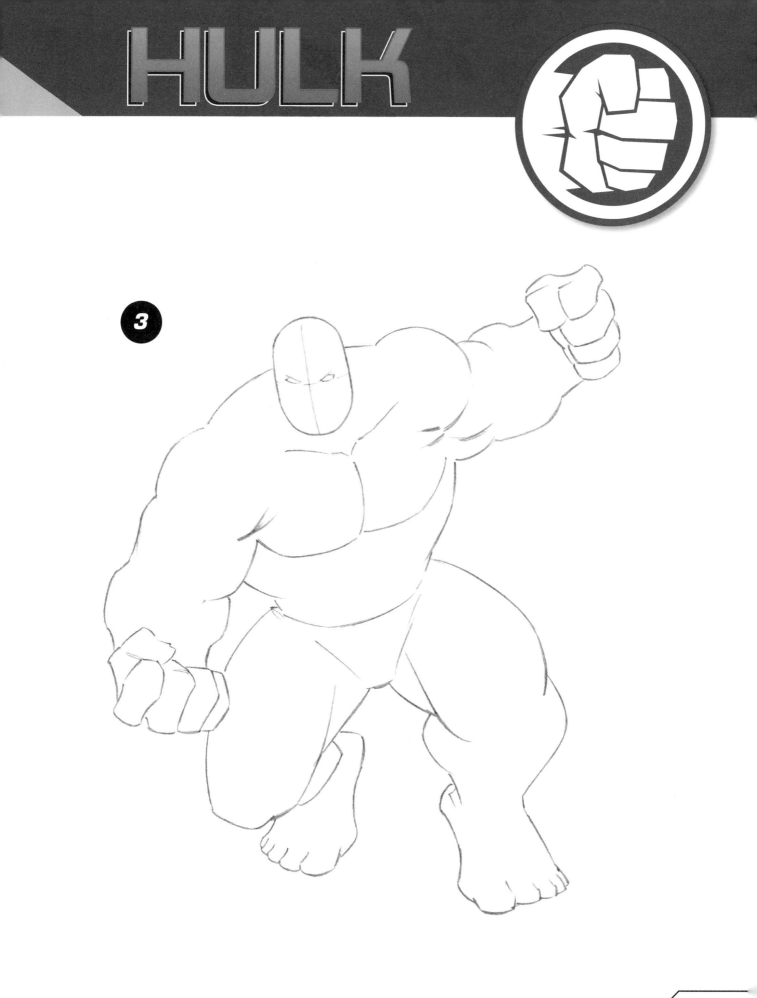

Bruce Banner's transformation into the Hulk is triggered by the release of adrenaline when he becomes excited.

6

7

THOR

Thor is the son of Odin. He wields one of the greatest weapons ever made, the enchanted hammer Mjolnir. Thor is smart, compassionate, self-assured, and would never stop fighting for a worthwhile cause.

Powers & Abilities

- Wields a powerful hammer forged from uru metal; the hammer cannot be used by anyone unworthy

- Can fly using Mjolnir

- Possesses the Belt of Strength and a pair of iron gauntlets to protect him while using Mjolnir

REAL NAME:
Thor Odinson

HEIGHT:
6'6"

WEIGHT:
640 lbs.

Follow along, first drawing basic shapes with light pencil lines. Copy the new lines shown in each step, eventually darkening the lines you want to keep and erasing the rest. Finally, add color to your drawing.

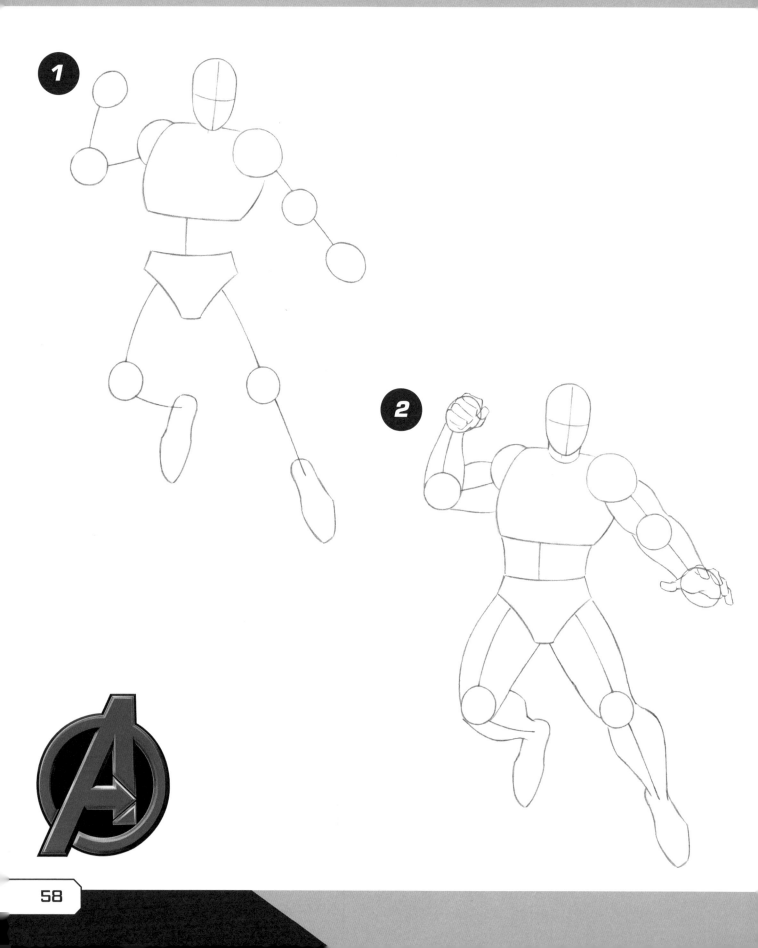

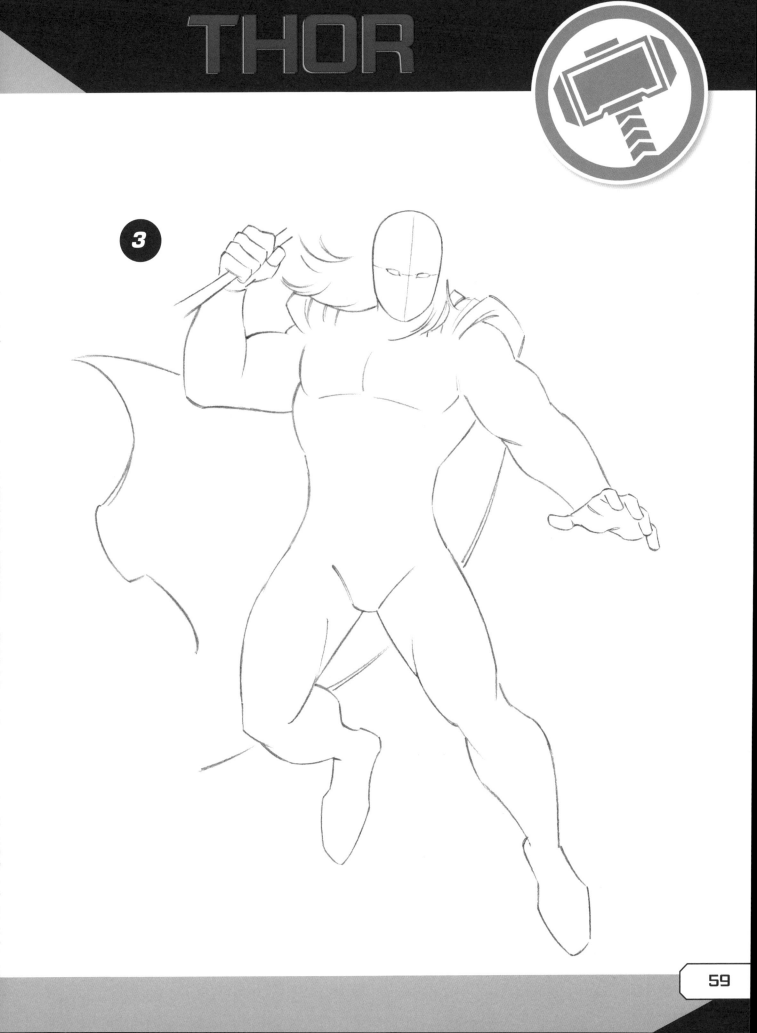

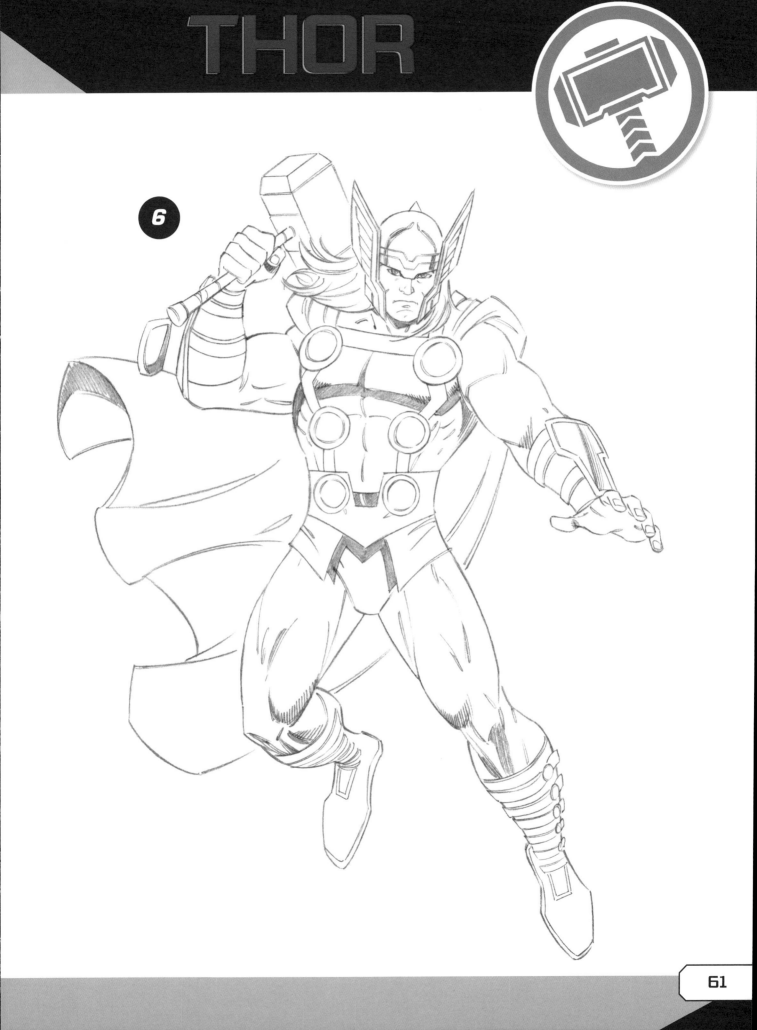

THE END

Also available from Walter Foster Jr.

**Learn to Draw
Marvel Avengers:
Mightiest Heroes Edition**
ISBN: 978-1-60058-829-7

**Learn to Draw
Marvel Spider-Man**
ISBN: 978-1-60058-832-7

**Learn to Draw
Marvel Spider-Man
Villains**
ISBN: 978-1-60058-835-8